GET IN TOUCH
Info@AfterThePitch.com

LOVE US OR THINK WE CAN DO BETTER?
Feedback@AfterThePitch.com

CREATED BY
Adrian T. Marable

Published by Beloda Media



Colarity.com
AfterThePitch.com

# To the entrepreneurs who aspire to change the world.

# Goodluck!

Welcome, entrepreneur!

You've taken the leap into pitching your business to investors. That's no small feat. Whether you're just starting out or you've already had a few pitches under your belt, you're here because you know how important it is to stay organized, learn from every experience, and keep improving. This book is here to help you do just that.

Let's face it, pitching can feel overwhelming. You're trying to impress investors, answer tough questions, and properly communicat your company's vision, all while hoping for a positive outcome. It's a lot to juggle. That's why this tracker exists. Think of it as your go-to tool for staying on top of your game.

Each pitch you make is an opportunity. It's not not just to secure funding, but to learn more about your business, refine your story, and build valuable relationships. The key is to document those experiences. By writing down the details of every pitch, you'll uncover patterns, identify what works (and what doesn't), and create a roadmap for your pitching journey.

This tracker is designed to make it simple. It's a two-page system. The first page is for recording the facts: who you pitched to, how it went, and what you need to do next. The second page? That's where the real magic happens. It's for your thoughts, reflections, and insights. What did you crush? What you can improve? How did the investor responded?

Think of this book as your pitch coach. It won't sit in the room with you, but it will prepare you for the next pitch and the one after that. With every entry, you'll become sharper, more confident, and better equipped to win over investors.

So grab a pen! Your big idea deserves funding. Let's document your way to making it happen!

You've got this. Let's go!!!

This tracker is your secret weapon for organizing, reflecting on, and improving your investor pitches. It's easy to use and designed to give you clarity at every step of the pitching process. Here's a quick guide to help you make the most of it:

**Step 1: Document the Basics**
After each pitch, take a few minutes to fill out the first page. This is where you capture the key details:

**Investor Name, Date, and Contact Info**: These ensure you can easily track who you pitched and follow up.

**Pitch Method and Duration**: Record how and where the pitch took place, along with how long it lasted. These are details that may help you notice patterns over time.

**Focus Area and Funding Size**: Write down the investor's area of interest (e.g., tech, healthcare) and their typical funding range to ensure alignment with your business.

**Interest Level**: Rate their initial reaction (Low, Medium, High) for a quick gauge of their enthusiasm.

**Feedback/Questions Asked**: Capture what they said or asked you. This is invaluable for refining your future pitches.

**Follow-Up Actions**: Note the next steps you need to take, whether it's sending additional documents, scheduling another meeting, or following up on feedback.

**Decision**: Mark the current status of the pitch (Accepted, Declined, Pending).

**Step 2: Reflect and Improve**
Turn to the second page for a deeper dive into your experience. This is where you can capture your thoughts and observations.

**What Went Well**: Highlight the parts of your pitch that stood out. Maybe your delivery was sharp, or they were excited about your business model.

**Investor Reactions**: Take note of how they responded to different parts of your pitch. This can help you fine-tune your approach.

**Areas for Improvement**: Be honest with yourself about what could have gone better. Did you stumble on a question? Were you unprepared for a certain topic? Use this space to learn and grow.

## Step 3: Track Networking Potential

Sometimes, even if an investor doesn't fund your business, they might connect you with others who can. Use the Networking Potential section to record any referrals, suggestions, or helpful connections they mentioned.

## Step 4: Keep Tabs on Documents Sent

Use the Documents Sent field to track what you've shared with the investor (like your pitch deck, financials, or follow-up emails) and when. This ensures nothing slips through the cracks.

## Step 5: Review Periodically

This tracker isn't just for one-time use. Over time, it becomes a powerful tool to identify trends and improve your pitching game. Review your completed entries regularly to:
    Spot recurring feedback or questions.
    Pinpoint which parts of your pitch resonate most.
    Recognize areas where you consistently need to improve.

By using this tracker consistently, you'll not only stay organized but also gain valuable insights to level up your pitching strategy. It's not just about tracking, it's about learning, improving, and securing the funding you and your business deserves.

You've got the vision; this tracker will help you refine it.

YOU GOT THIS!!!

# The Benefits of Documenting Your Pitches

Let's talk about why documenting your pitches is one of the smartest moves you can make on your journey to securing funding. Sure, it might feel like "just another task," but trust me, it's so much more than that.

Here's the thing: every pitch is a learning experience. Whether the outcome is a "yes," a "no," or a "let's talk later," there's valuable insight to be gained. But here's the catch: if you don't write it down, those details can slip away faster than you'd think. By documenting your pitches, you're setting yourself up for long-term success.

### 1. Stay Organized

When you're pitching to multiple investors, keeping track of who you spoke to, what you discussed, and what they want next is critical. Did they ask for your financials? Were they excited about a specific part of your pitch? Did they mention someone you should meet? Writing it down ensures nothing gets lost in the shuffle.

### 2. Spot Patterns in Feedback

Investors are great at pointing out what they like and what they don't. When you track their questions and comments, you'll start to notice patterns. Maybe multiple investors ask about your market research or scaling plans. That's a sign you might need to refine that part of your pitch.

### 3. Build Better Relationships

Investors remember entrepreneurs who pay attention. Documenting your pitches shows you're serious, professional, and focused. Plus, when you follow up with tailored messages or bring up something they mentioned, you'll stand out as someone who listens and takes action.

## 4. Measure Your Progress

Tracking your pitches helps you see how far you've come. At first, you might stumble over tough questions or feel nervous, but over time, you'll notice your confidence and clarity improving. Those small wins add up, and having a record of them is a great motivator.

## 5. Refine Your Strategy

Every pitch teaches you something about your approach, your investors, and even your business. When you document each experience, you can reflect on what worked, what didn't, and how you can improve. It's like having a playbook for your success.

## 6. Strengthen Your Follow-Up Game

Following up is where deals are often won or lost. When you document what an investor wants or expects, you can follow through with exactly what they need. It could be sending your pitch deck, providing additional information, or just staying in touch.

## 7. Keep Networking Opportunities Alive

Sometimes an investor might not fund you, but they could introduce you to someone who will. By writing down any suggested connections or resources, you're ensuring you don't miss out on those golden opportunities.

## 8. Create a Legacy of Lessons Learned

Imagine looking back a year from now with a detailed record of every pitch you've made. That's not just helpful, it's powerful. Your documented pitches become a treasure trove of insights you can share with your team, use to mentor others, or reflect on as you grow.

Documenting your pitches is about both tracking and building a foundation for success. It helps you improve, connect, and turn those investor meetings into funding for your vision. Now, grab your pen and let's make it happen. Your future self (and your business) will thank you for it!

# Tips for an Effective Pitch

Pitching your business to investors can feel like stepping onto a stage. Your goal is to captivate, convince, and leave a lasting impression. While every pitch is unique, there are some universal strategies that can help you shine. Here's a straightforward guide to nailing your next pitch and getting one step closer to securing funding.

## Know Your Audience

Before you pitch, do your homework. Learn about the investor's interests, previous investments, and areas of expertise. Tailor your pitch to align with their priorities. The more personalized your approach, the more likely they'll feel you're the right fit.

## Start Strong

First impressions matter. Begin with a compelling hook; a surprising fact, a bold statement, or a personal story that ties into your business. Grab their attention from the first moment and set the tone for an engaging presentation.

## Be Clear and Concise

Investors don't want a deep dive into every detail of your business. They want a high-level overview that's easy to follow. Focus on the problem you're solving, how your business is the solution, and why it's a great investment. Stick to the highlights, and save the nitty-gritty for follow-up discussions.

## Tell a Story

Numbers and data are important, but people connect with stories. Share the "why" behind your business. What inspired you to start it? How does it impact people's lives? A well-told story can make your pitch memorable and relatable.

## Highlight Your Value Proposition

What makes your business unique? Why should investors choose you over others? Be crystal clear about your competitive advantage and how it sets you apart in the market.

## Know Your Numbers

Confidence in your financials is a must. Be prepared to discuss revenue, profit margins, market size, and projections. If you don't know your numbers, it sends a red flag to investors. Practice explaining your data in simple, compelling terms.

## Anticipate Questions

Investors will ask tough questions because that's their job. Think ahead and prepare answers for common concerns, like scalability, market competition, and risk factors. The more confident and thoughtful your responses, the more trust you'll build.

## Show Passion

Investors want to back people who believe in their vision. Speak with genuine excitement about your business and its potential. Passion is contagious, and it shows that you're personally invested in the success of your venture.

## Keep Visuals Clean

If you're using slides or a pitch deck, make sure they're simple, visually appealing, and easy to read. Avoid cluttered layouts or excessive text. Your visuals should support your story, not distract from it.

## End with a Clear Ask

What do you want from the investor? Be specific. Whether it's a funding amount, a connection, or advice, spell it out clearly at the end of your pitch. A strong and direct ask shows confidence and focus.

## Follow Up

The pitch doesn't end when the meeting does. Send a thank-you note and follow up with any promised materials or answers to questions. Stay on their radar with timely and professional communication.

**Practice, Practice, Practice**
The best pitches come from preparation. Rehearse your pitch until it feels natural and you can deliver it with confidence. Practice in front of friends, mentors, or even a mirror to fine-tune your delivery.

Pitching is an art and a skill. The more you prepare and refine your approach, the better chances you have of making a lasting impression. Remember, every pitch is an opportunity to grow, learn, and move closer to achieving your goals.

INVESTOR NAME:                                                    DATE:

CONTACT INFORMATION:

PITCH METHOD: IN-PERSON    VIRTUAL    PHONE CALL    EMAIL

PITCH DURATION:

FOCUS AREA:

FUNDING SIZE:

PREVIOUS INVESTMENTS:

INTEREST LEVE: LOW    MEDIUM    HIGH

FOLLOW-UP ACTIONS:




FEEDBACK/QUESTIONS ASKED:




DECISION: ACCEPTED    DECLINED    PENDING

KEY TAKEAWAYS: INSIGHTS ABOUT THE INVESTOR OR THEIR PREFERENCES.




NETWORKING POTENTIAL: DID THEY SUGGEST CONNECTIONS TO OTHER INVESTORS OR RESOURCES?




DOCUMENTS SENT: (E.G., PITCH DECK, FINANCIALS) AND DATE SENT.

# NOTES & THOUGHTS

INVESTOR NAME:                                    DATE:

CONTACT INFORMATION:

PITCH METHOD: IN-PERSON    VIRTUAL    PHONE CALL    EMAIL

PITCH DURATION:

FOCUS AREA:

FUNDING SIZE:

PREVIOUS INVESTMENTS:

INTEREST LEVE: LOW    MEDIUM    HIGH

FOLLOW-UP ACTIONS:




FEEDBACK/QUESTIONS ASKED:




DECISION: ACCEPTED    DECLINED    PENDING

KEY TAKEAWAYS: INSIGHTS ABOUT THE INVESTOR OR THEIR
PREFERENCES.




NETWORKING POTENTIAL: DID THEY SUGGEST CONNECTIONS TO
OTHER INVESTORS OR RESOURCES?




DOCUMENTS SENT: (E.G., PITCH DECK, FINANCIALS) AND DATE SENT.

# NOTES & THOUGHTS

INVESTOR NAME:                                    DATE:

CONTACT INFORMATION:

PITCH METHOD: IN-PERSON    VIRTUAL    PHONE CALL    EMAIL

PITCH DURATION:

FOCUS AREA:

FUNDING SIZE:

PREVIOUS INVESTMENTS:

INTEREST LEVE: LOW    MEDIUM    HIGH

FOLLOW-UP ACTIONS:


FEEDBACK/QUESTIONS ASKED:


DECISION: ACCEPTED    DECLINED    PENDING

KEY TAKEAWAYS: INSIGHTS ABOUT THE INVESTOR OR THEIR PREFERENCES.


NETWORKING POTENTIAL: DID THEY SUGGEST CONNECTIONS TO OTHER INVESTORS OR RESOURCES?


DOCUMENTS SENT: (E.G., PITCH DECK, FINANCIALS) AND DATE SENT.

# NOTES & THOUGHTS

INVESTOR NAME:                                                    DATE:

CONTACT INFORMATION:

PITCH METHOD: IN-PERSON    VIRTUAL    PHONE CALL    EMAIL

PITCH DURATION:

FOCUS AREA:

FUNDING SIZE:

PREVIOUS INVESTMENTS:

INTEREST LEVE: LOW    MEDIUM    HIGH

FOLLOW-UP ACTIONS:


FEEDBACK/QUESTIONS ASKED:


DECISION: ACCEPTED    DECLINED    PENDING

KEY TAKEAWAYS: INSIGHTS ABOUT THE INVESTOR OR THEIR PREFERENCES.


NETWORKING POTENTIAL: DID THEY SUGGEST CONNECTIONS TO OTHER INVESTORS OR RESOURCES?


DOCUMENTS SENT: (E.G., PITCH DECK, FINANCIALS) AND DATE SENT.

# NOTES & THOUGHTS

INVESTOR NAME:                                    DATE:

CONTACT INFORMATION:

PITCH METHOD: IN-PERSON    VIRTUAL    PHONE CALL    EMAIL

PITCH DURATION:

FOCUS AREA:

FUNDING SIZE:

PREVIOUS INVESTMENTS:

INTEREST LEVE: LOW    MEDIUM    HIGH

FOLLOW-UP ACTIONS:


FEEDBACK/QUESTIONS ASKED:


DECISION: ACCEPTED    DECLINED    PENDING

KEY TAKEAWAYS: INSIGHTS ABOUT THE INVESTOR OR THEIR PREFERENCES.




NETWORKING POTENTIAL: DID THEY SUGGEST CONNECTIONS TO OTHER INVESTORS OR RESOURCES?


DOCUMENTS SENT: (E.G., PITCH DECK, FINANCIALS) AND DATE SENT.

# NOTES & THOUGHTS

INVESTOR NAME:                                         DATE:

CONTACT INFORMATION:

PITCH METHOD: IN-PERSON    VIRTUAL    PHONE CALL    EMAIL

PITCH DURATION:

FOCUS AREA:

FUNDING SIZE:

PREVIOUS INVESTMENTS:

INTEREST LEVE: LOW    MEDIUM    HIGH

FOLLOW-UP ACTIONS:



FEEDBACK/QUESTIONS ASKED:



DECISION: ACCEPTED    DECLINED    PENDING

KEY TAKEAWAYS: INSIGHTS ABOUT THE INVESTOR OR THEIR PREFERENCES.



NETWORKING POTENTIAL: DID THEY SUGGEST CONNECTIONS TO OTHER INVESTORS OR RESOURCES?



DOCUMENTS SENT: (E.G., PITCH DECK, FINANCIALS) AND DATE SENT.

INVESTOR NAME:                                           DATE:

CONTACT INFORMATION:

PITCH METHOD: IN-PERSON    VIRTUAL    PHONE CALL    EMAIL

PITCH DURATION:

FOCUS AREA:

FUNDING SIZE:

PREVIOUS INVESTMENTS:

INTEREST LEVE: LOW    MEDIUM    HIGH

FOLLOW-UP ACTIONS:

FEEDBACK/QUESTIONS ASKED:

DECISION: ACCEPTED    DECLINED    PENDING

KEY TAKEAWAYS: INSIGHTS ABOUT THE INVESTOR OR THEIR PREFERENCES.

NETWORKING POTENTIAL: DID THEY SUGGEST CONNECTIONS TO OTHER INVESTORS OR RESOURCES?

DOCUMENTS SENT: (E.G., PITCH DECK, FINANCIALS) AND DATE SENT.

# NOTES & THOUGHTS

INVESTOR NAME:                                          DATE:

CONTACT INFORMATION:

PITCH METHOD: IN-PERSON    VIRTUAL    PHONE CALL    EMAIL

PITCH DURATION:

FOCUS AREA:

FUNDING SIZE:

PREVIOUS INVESTMENTS:

INTEREST LEVE: LOW    MEDIUM    HIGH

FOLLOW-UP ACTIONS:

FEEDBACK/QUESTIONS ASKED:

DECISION: ACCEPTED    DECLINED    PENDING

KEY TAKEAWAYS: INSIGHTS ABOUT THE INVESTOR OR THEIR PREFERENCES.

NETWORKING POTENTIAL: DID THEY SUGGEST CONNECTIONS TO OTHER INVESTORS OR RESOURCES?

DOCUMENTS SENT: (E.G., PITCH DECK, FINANCIALS) AND DATE SENT.

INVESTOR NAME:                                                    DATE:

CONTACT INFORMATION:

PITCH METHOD: IN-PERSON    VIRTUAL    PHONE CALL    EMAIL

PITCH DURATION:

FOCUS AREA:

FUNDING SIZE:

PREVIOUS INVESTMENTS:

INTEREST LEVE: LOW    MEDIUM    HIGH

FOLLOW-UP ACTIONS:




FEEDBACK/QUESTIONS ASKED:




DECISION: ACCEPTED    DECLINED    PENDING

KEY TAKEAWAYS: INSIGHTS ABOUT THE INVESTOR OR THEIR PREFERENCES.




NETWORKING POTENTIAL: DID THEY SUGGEST CONNECTIONS TO OTHER INVESTORS OR RESOURCES?




DOCUMENTS SENT: (E.G., PITCH DECK, FINANCIALS) AND DATE SENT.

# NOTES & THOUGHTS

INVESTOR NAME:                                    DATE:

CONTACT INFORMATION:

PITCH METHOD: IN-PERSON    VIRTUAL    PHONE CALL    EMAIL

PITCH DURATION:

FOCUS AREA:

FUNDING SIZE:

PREVIOUS INVESTMENTS:

INTEREST LEVE: LOW    MEDIUM    HIGH

FOLLOW-UP ACTIONS:


FEEDBACK/QUESTIONS ASKED:


DECISION: ACCEPTED    DECLINED    PENDING

KEY TAKEAWAYS: INSIGHTS ABOUT THE INVESTOR OR THEIR PREFERENCES.




NETWORKING POTENTIAL: DID THEY SUGGEST CONNECTIONS TO OTHER INVESTORS OR RESOURCES?



DOCUMENTS SENT: (E.G., PITCH DECK, FINANCIALS) AND DATE SENT.

# NOTES & THOUGHTS

INVESTOR NAME:                                          DATE:

CONTACT INFORMATION:

PITCH METHOD: IN-PERSON    VIRTUAL    PHONE CALL    EMAIL

PITCH DURATION:

FOCUS AREA:

FUNDING SIZE:

PREVIOUS INVESTMENTS:

INTEREST LEVE: LOW    MEDIUM    HIGH

FOLLOW-UP ACTIONS:


FEEDBACK/QUESTIONS ASKED:


DECISION: ACCEPTED    DECLINED    PENDING

KEY TAKEAWAYS: INSIGHTS ABOUT THE INVESTOR OR THEIR PREFERENCES.


NETWORKING POTENTIAL: DID THEY SUGGEST CONNECTIONS TO OTHER INVESTORS OR RESOURCES?


DOCUMENTS SENT: (E.G., PITCH DECK, FINANCIALS) AND DATE SENT.

# NOTES & THOUGHTS

INVESTOR NAME:                                    DATE:

CONTACT INFORMATION:

PITCH METHOD: IN-PERSON    VIRTUAL    PHONE CALL    EMAIL

PITCH DURATION:

FOCUS AREA:

FUNDING SIZE:

PREVIOUS INVESTMENTS:

INTEREST LEVE: LOW    MEDIUM    HIGH

FOLLOW-UP ACTIONS:

FEEDBACK/QUESTIONS ASKED:

DECISION: ACCEPTED    DECLINED    PENDING

KEY TAKEAWAYS: INSIGHTS ABOUT THE INVESTOR OR THEIR PREFERENCES.

NETWORKING POTENTIAL: DID THEY SUGGEST CONNECTIONS TO OTHER INVESTORS OR RESOURCES?

DOCUMENTS SENT: (E.G., PITCH DECK, FINANCIALS) AND DATE SENT.

# NOTES & THOUGHTS

INVESTOR NAME:                                          DATE:

CONTACT INFORMATION:

PITCH METHOD: IN-PERSON    VIRTUAL    PHONE CALL    EMAIL

PITCH DURATION:

FOCUS AREA:

FUNDING SIZE:

PREVIOUS INVESTMENTS:

INTEREST LEVE: LOW    MEDIUM    HIGH

FOLLOW-UP ACTIONS:

FEEDBACK/QUESTIONS ASKED:

DECISION: ACCEPTED    DECLINED    PENDING

KEY TAKEAWAYS: INSIGHTS ABOUT THE INVESTOR OR THEIR PREFERENCES.

NETWORKING POTENTIAL: DID THEY SUGGEST CONNECTIONS TO OTHER INVESTORS OR RESOURCES?

DOCUMENTS SENT: (E.G., PITCH DECK, FINANCIALS) AND DATE SENT.

# NOTES & THOUGHTS

INVESTOR NAME:                                               DATE:

CONTACT INFORMATION:

PITCH METHOD: IN-PERSON    VIRTUAL    PHONE CALL    EMAIL

PITCH DURATION:

FOCUS AREA:

FUNDING SIZE:

PREVIOUS INVESTMENTS:

INTEREST LEVE: LOW    MEDIUM    HIGH

FOLLOW-UP ACTIONS:


FEEDBACK/QUESTIONS ASKED:


DECISION: ACCEPTED    DECLINED    PENDING

KEY TAKEAWAYS: INSIGHTS ABOUT THE INVESTOR OR THEIR PREFERENCES.




NETWORKING POTENTIAL: DID THEY SUGGEST CONNECTIONS TO OTHER INVESTORS OR RESOURCES?



DOCUMENTS SENT: (E.G., PITCH DECK, FINANCIALS) AND DATE SENT.

INVESTOR NAME:                                              DATE:

CONTACT INFORMATION:

PITCH METHOD: IN-PERSON    VIRTUAL    PHONE CALL    EMAIL

PITCH DURATION:

FOCUS AREA:

FUNDING SIZE:

PREVIOUS INVESTMENTS:

INTEREST LEVE: LOW    MEDIUM    HIGH

FOLLOW-UP ACTIONS:


FEEDBACK/QUESTIONS ASKED:


DECISION: ACCEPTED    DECLINED    PENDING

KEY TAKEAWAYS: INSIGHTS ABOUT THE INVESTOR OR THEIR PREFERENCES.


NETWORKING POTENTIAL: DID THEY SUGGEST CONNECTIONS TO OTHER INVESTORS OR RESOURCES?


DOCUMENTS SENT: (E.G., PITCH DECK, FINANCIALS) AND DATE SENT.

## NOTES & THOUGHTS

INVESTOR NAME:                        DATE:

CONTACT INFORMATION:

PITCH METHOD: IN-PERSON     VIRTUAL     PHONE CALL     EMAIL

PITCH DURATION:

FOCUS AREA:

FUNDING SIZE:

PREVIOUS INVESTMENTS:

INTEREST LEVE: LOW     MEDIUM     HIGH

FOLLOW-UP ACTIONS:




FEEDBACK/QUESTIONS ASKED:




DECISION: ACCEPTED     DECLINED     PENDING

KEY TAKEAWAYS: INSIGHTS ABOUT THE INVESTOR OR THEIR PREFERENCES.




NETWORKING POTENTIAL: DID THEY SUGGEST CONNECTIONS TO OTHER INVESTORS OR RESOURCES?




DOCUMENTS SENT: (E.G., PITCH DECK, FINANCIALS) AND DATE SENT.

# NOTES & THOUGHTS

INVESTOR NAME:                                          DATE:

CONTACT INFORMATION:

PITCH METHOD: IN-PERSON    VIRTUAL    PHONE CALL    EMAIL

PITCH DURATION:

FOCUS AREA:

FUNDING SIZE:

PREVIOUS INVESTMENTS:

INTEREST LEVE: LOW    MEDIUM    HIGH

FOLLOW-UP ACTIONS:


FEEDBACK/QUESTIONS ASKED:


DECISION: ACCEPTED    DECLINED    PENDING

KEY TAKEAWAYS: INSIGHTS ABOUT THE INVESTOR OR THEIR PREFERENCES.




NETWORKING POTENTIAL: DID THEY SUGGEST CONNECTIONS TO OTHER INVESTORS OR RESOURCES?


DOCUMENTS SENT: (E.G., PITCH DECK, FINANCIALS) AND DATE SENT.

# NOTES & THOUGHTS

INVESTOR NAME: DATE:

CONTACT INFORMATION:

PITCH METHOD: IN-PERSON   VIRTUAL   PHONE CALL   EMAIL

PITCH DURATION:

FOCUS AREA:

FUNDING SIZE:

PREVIOUS INVESTMENTS:

INTEREST LEVE: LOW   MEDIUM   HIGH

FOLLOW-UP ACTIONS:

FEEDBACK/QUESTIONS ASKED:

DECISION: ACCEPTED   DECLINED   PENDING

KEY TAKEAWAYS: INSIGHTS ABOUT THE INVESTOR OR THEIR PREFERENCES.

NETWORKING POTENTIAL: DID THEY SUGGEST CONNECTIONS TO OTHER INVESTORS OR RESOURCES?

DOCUMENTS SENT: (E.G., PITCH DECK, FINANCIALS) AND DATE SENT.

# NOTES & THOUGHTS

INVESTOR NAME:                                        DATE:

CONTACT INFORMATION:

PITCH METHOD: IN-PERSON    VIRTUAL    PHONE CALL    EMAIL

PITCH DURATION:

FOCUS AREA:

FUNDING SIZE:

PREVIOUS INVESTMENTS:

INTEREST LEVE: LOW    MEDIUM    HIGH

FOLLOW-UP ACTIONS:


FEEDBACK/QUESTIONS ASKED:


DECISION: ACCEPTED    DECLINED    PENDING

KEY TAKEAWAYS: INSIGHTS ABOUT THE INVESTOR OR THEIR PREFERENCES.




NETWORKING POTENTIAL: DID THEY SUGGEST CONNECTIONS TO OTHER INVESTORS OR RESOURCES?



DOCUMENTS SENT: (E.G., PITCH DECK, FINANCIALS) AND DATE SENT.

# NOTES & THOUGHTS

INVESTOR NAME:                                    DATE:

CONTACT INFORMATION:

PITCH METHOD: IN-PERSON    VIRTUAL    PHONE CALL    EMAIL

PITCH DURATION:

FOCUS AREA:

FUNDING SIZE:

PREVIOUS INVESTMENTS:

INTEREST LEVE: LOW    MEDIUM    HIGH

FOLLOW-UP ACTIONS:

FEEDBACK/QUESTIONS ASKED:

DECISION: ACCEPTED    DECLINED    PENDING

KEY TAKEAWAYS: INSIGHTS ABOUT THE INVESTOR OR THEIR PREFERENCES.

NETWORKING POTENTIAL: DID THEY SUGGEST CONNECTIONS TO OTHER INVESTORS OR RESOURCES?

DOCUMENTS SENT: (E.G., PITCH DECK, FINANCIALS) AND DATE SENT.

# NOTES & THOUGHTS

INVESTOR NAME:                                        DATE:

CONTACT INFORMATION:

PITCH METHOD: IN-PERSON    VIRTUAL    PHONE CALL    EMAIL

PITCH DURATION:

FOCUS AREA:

FUNDING SIZE:

PREVIOUS INVESTMENTS:

INTEREST LEVE: LOW    MEDIUM    HIGH

FOLLOW-UP ACTIONS:


FEEDBACK/QUESTIONS ASKED:


DECISION: ACCEPTED    DECLINED    PENDING

KEY TAKEAWAYS: INSIGHTS ABOUT THE INVESTOR OR THEIR PREFERENCES.

NETWORKING POTENTIAL: DID THEY SUGGEST CONNECTIONS TO OTHER INVESTORS OR RESOURCES?

DOCUMENTS SENT: (E.G., PITCH DECK, FINANCIALS) AND DATE SENT.

# NOTES & THOUGHTS

INVESTOR NAME:                                    DATE:

CONTACT INFORMATION:

PITCH METHOD: IN-PERSON     VIRTUAL     PHONE CALL     EMAIL

PITCH DURATION:

FOCUS AREA:

FUNDING SIZE:

PREVIOUS INVESTMENTS:

INTEREST LEVE: LOW     MEDIUM     HIGH

FOLLOW-UP ACTIONS:


FEEDBACK/QUESTIONS ASKED:


DECISION: ACCEPTED     DECLINED     PENDING

KEY TAKEAWAYS: INSIGHTS ABOUT THE INVESTOR OR THEIR PREFERENCES.


NETWORKING POTENTIAL: DID THEY SUGGEST CONNECTIONS TO OTHER INVESTORS OR RESOURCES?


DOCUMENTS SENT: (E.G., PITCH DECK, FINANCIALS) AND DATE SENT.

# NOTES & THOUGHTS

INVESTOR NAME:                                        DATE:

CONTACT INFORMATION:

PITCH METHOD: IN-PERSON    VIRTUAL    PHONE CALL    EMAIL

PITCH DURATION:

FOCUS AREA:

FUNDING SIZE:

PREVIOUS INVESTMENTS:

INTEREST LEVE: LOW    MEDIUM    HIGH

FOLLOW-UP ACTIONS:

FEEDBACK/QUESTIONS ASKED:

DECISION: ACCEPTED    DECLINED    PENDING

KEY TAKEAWAYS: INSIGHTS ABOUT THE INVESTOR OR THEIR PREFERENCES.

NETWORKING POTENTIAL: DID THEY SUGGEST CONNECTIONS TO OTHER INVESTORS OR RESOURCES?

DOCUMENTS SENT: (E.G., PITCH DECK, FINANCIALS) AND DATE SENT.

# NOTES & THOUGHTS

INVESTOR NAME:                                        DATE:

CONTACT INFORMATION:

PITCH METHOD: IN-PERSON    VIRTUAL    PHONE CALL    EMAIL

PITCH DURATION:

FOCUS AREA:

FUNDING SIZE:

PREVIOUS INVESTMENTS:

INTEREST LEVE: LOW    MEDIUM    HIGH

FOLLOW-UP ACTIONS:


FEEDBACK/QUESTIONS ASKED:


DECISION: ACCEPTED    DECLINED    PENDING

KEY TAKEAWAYS: INSIGHTS ABOUT THE INVESTOR OR THEIR PREFERENCES.


NETWORKING POTENTIAL: DID THEY SUGGEST CONNECTIONS TO OTHER INVESTORS OR RESOURCES?


DOCUMENTS SENT: (E.G., PITCH DECK, FINANCIALS) AND DATE SENT.

# NOTES & THOUGHTS

INVESTOR NAME:                                                    DATE:

CONTACT INFORMATION:

PITCH METHOD: IN-PERSON    VIRTUAL    PHONE CALL    EMAIL

PITCH DURATION:

FOCUS AREA:

FUNDING SIZE:

PREVIOUS INVESTMENTS:

INTEREST LEVE: LOW    MEDIUM    HIGH

FOLLOW-UP ACTIONS:



FEEDBACK/QUESTIONS ASKED:



DECISION: ACCEPTED    DECLINED    PENDING

KEY TAKEAWAYS: INSIGHTS ABOUT THE INVESTOR OR THEIR PREFERENCES.



NETWORKING POTENTIAL: DID THEY SUGGEST CONNECTIONS TO OTHER INVESTORS OR RESOURCES?



DOCUMENTS SENT: (E.G., PITCH DECK, FINANCIALS) AND DATE SENT.

# NOTES & THOUGHTS

INVESTOR NAME:                                          DATE:

CONTACT INFORMATION:

PITCH METHOD: IN-PERSON    VIRTUAL    PHONE CALL    EMAIL

PITCH DURATION:

FOCUS AREA:

FUNDING SIZE:

PREVIOUS INVESTMENTS:

INTEREST LEVE: LOW    MEDIUM    HIGH

FOLLOW-UP ACTIONS:


FEEDBACK/QUESTIONS ASKED:


DECISION: ACCEPTED    DECLINED    PENDING

KEY TAKEAWAYS: INSIGHTS ABOUT THE INVESTOR OR THEIR PREFERENCES.


NETWORKING POTENTIAL: DID THEY SUGGEST CONNECTIONS TO OTHER INVESTORS OR RESOURCES?


DOCUMENTS SENT: (E.G., PITCH DECK, FINANCIALS) AND DATE SENT.

# NOTES & THOUGHTS

INVESTOR NAME:                                      DATE:

CONTACT INFORMATION:

PITCH METHOD: IN-PERSON    VIRTUAL    PHONE CALL    EMAIL

PITCH DURATION:

FOCUS AREA:

FUNDING SIZE:

PREVIOUS INVESTMENTS:

INTEREST LEVE: LOW    MEDIUM    HIGH

FOLLOW-UP ACTIONS:



FEEDBACK/QUESTIONS ASKED:



DECISION: ACCEPTED    DECLINED    PENDING

KEY TAKEAWAYS: INSIGHTS ABOUT THE INVESTOR OR THEIR PREFERENCES.



NETWORKING POTENTIAL: DID THEY SUGGEST CONNECTIONS TO OTHER INVESTORS OR RESOURCES?



DOCUMENTS SENT: (E.G., PITCH DECK, FINANCIALS) AND DATE SENT.

# NOTES & THOUGHTS

INVESTOR NAME:                                                    DATE:

CONTACT INFORMATION:

PITCH METHOD: IN-PERSON     VIRTUAL     PHONE CALL     EMAIL

PITCH DURATION:

FOCUS AREA:

FUNDING SIZE:

PREVIOUS INVESTMENTS:

INTEREST LEVE: LOW     MEDIUM     HIGH

FOLLOW-UP ACTIONS:




FEEDBACK/QUESTIONS ASKED:




DECISION: ACCEPTED     DECLINED     PENDING

KEY TAKEAWAYS: INSIGHTS ABOUT THE INVESTOR OR THEIR
PREFERENCES.




NETWORKING POTENTIAL: DID THEY SUGGEST CONNECTIONS TO
OTHER INVESTORS OR RESOURCES?




DOCUMENTS SENT: (E.G., PITCH DECK, FINANCIALS) AND DATE SENT.

INVESTOR NAME:                                          DATE:

CONTACT INFORMATION:

PITCH METHOD: IN-PERSON    VIRTUAL    PHONE CALL    EMAIL

PITCH DURATION:

FOCUS AREA:

FUNDING SIZE:

PREVIOUS INVESTMENTS:

INTEREST LEVE: LOW    MEDIUM    HIGH

FOLLOW-UP ACTIONS:


FEEDBACK/QUESTIONS ASKED:


DECISION: ACCEPTED    DECLINED    PENDING

KEY TAKEAWAYS: INSIGHTS ABOUT THE INVESTOR OR THEIR PREFERENCES.

NETWORKING POTENTIAL: DID THEY SUGGEST CONNECTIONS TO OTHER INVESTORS OR RESOURCES?

DOCUMENTS SENT: (E.G., PITCH DECK, FINANCIALS) AND DATE SENT.

# NOTES & THOUGHTS

INVESTOR NAME:                                          DATE:

CONTACT INFORMATION:

PITCH METHOD: IN-PERSON    VIRTUAL    PHONE CALL    EMAIL

PITCH DURATION:

FOCUS AREA:

FUNDING SIZE:

PREVIOUS INVESTMENTS:

INTEREST LEVE: LOW    MEDIUM    HIGH

FOLLOW-UP ACTIONS:


FEEDBACK/QUESTIONS ASKED:


DECISION: ACCEPTED    DECLINED    PENDING

KEY TAKEAWAYS: INSIGHTS ABOUT THE INVESTOR OR THEIR PREFERENCES.




NETWORKING POTENTIAL: DID THEY SUGGEST CONNECTIONS TO OTHER INVESTORS OR RESOURCES?



DOCUMENTS SENT: (E.G., PITCH DECK, FINANCIALS) AND DATE SENT.

# NOTES & THOUGHTS

INVESTOR NAME:                                          DATE:

CONTACT INFORMATION:

PITCH METHOD: IN-PERSON    VIRTUAL    PHONE CALL    EMAIL

PITCH DURATION:

FOCUS AREA:

FUNDING SIZE:

PREVIOUS INVESTMENTS:

INTEREST LEVE: LOW    MEDIUM    HIGH

FOLLOW-UP ACTIONS:


FEEDBACK/QUESTIONS ASKED:


DECISION: ACCEPTED    DECLINED    PENDING

KEY TAKEAWAYS: INSIGHTS ABOUT THE INVESTOR OR THEIR PREFERENCES.


NETWORKING POTENTIAL: DID THEY SUGGEST CONNECTIONS TO OTHER INVESTORS OR RESOURCES?


DOCUMENTS SENT: (E.G., PITCH DECK, FINANCIALS) AND DATE SENT.

# NOTES & THOUGHTS

INVESTOR NAME:                                         DATE:

CONTACT INFORMATION:

PITCH METHOD: IN-PERSON    VIRTUAL    PHONE CALL    EMAIL

PITCH DURATION:

FOCUS AREA:

FUNDING SIZE:

PREVIOUS INVESTMENTS:

INTEREST LEVE: LOW    MEDIUM    HIGH

FOLLOW-UP ACTIONS:




FEEDBACK/QUESTIONS ASKED:




DECISION: ACCEPTED    DECLINED    PENDING

KEY TAKEAWAYS: INSIGHTS ABOUT THE INVESTOR OR THEIR PREFERENCES.




NETWORKING POTENTIAL: DID THEY SUGGEST CONNECTIONS TO OTHER INVESTORS OR RESOURCES?




DOCUMENTS SENT: (E.G., PITCH DECK, FINANCIALS) AND DATE SENT.

# NOTES & THOUGHTS

INVESTOR NAME:                                    DATE:

CONTACT INFORMATION:

PITCH METHOD: IN-PERSON    VIRTUAL    PHONE CALL    EMAIL

PITCH DURATION:

FOCUS AREA:

FUNDING SIZE:

PREVIOUS INVESTMENTS:

INTEREST LEVE: LOW    MEDIUM    HIGH

FOLLOW-UP ACTIONS:




FEEDBACK/QUESTIONS ASKED:




DECISION: ACCEPTED    DECLINED    PENDING

KEY TAKEAWAYS: INSIGHTS ABOUT THE INVESTOR OR THEIR PREFERENCES.




NETWORKING POTENTIAL: DID THEY SUGGEST CONNECTIONS TO OTHER INVESTORS OR RESOURCES?




DOCUMENTS SENT: (E.G., PITCH DECK, FINANCIALS) AND DATE SENT.

# NOTES & THOUGHTS

INVESTOR NAME:                                                                DATE:

CONTACT INFORMATION:

PITCH METHOD: IN-PERSON    VIRTUAL    PHONE CALL    EMAIL

PITCH DURATION:

FOCUS AREA:

FUNDING SIZE:

PREVIOUS INVESTMENTS:

INTEREST LEVE: LOW    MEDIUM    HIGH

FOLLOW-UP ACTIONS:


FEEDBACK/QUESTIONS ASKED:


DECISION: ACCEPTED    DECLINED    PENDING

KEY TAKEAWAYS: INSIGHTS ABOUT THE INVESTOR OR THEIR PREFERENCES.


NETWORKING POTENTIAL: DID THEY SUGGEST CONNECTIONS TO OTHER INVESTORS OR RESOURCES?


DOCUMENTS SENT: (E.G., PITCH DECK, FINANCIALS) AND DATE SENT.

# NOTES & THOUGHTS

INVESTOR NAME:                                    DATE:

CONTACT INFORMATION:

PITCH METHOD: IN-PERSON    VIRTUAL    PHONE CALL    EMAIL

PITCH DURATION:

FOCUS AREA:

FUNDING SIZE:

PREVIOUS INVESTMENTS:

INTEREST LEVE: LOW    MEDIUM    HIGH

FOLLOW-UP ACTIONS:

FEEDBACK/QUESTIONS ASKED:

DECISION: ACCEPTED    DECLINED    PENDING

KEY TAKEAWAYS: INSIGHTS ABOUT THE INVESTOR OR THEIR PREFERENCES.

NETWORKING POTENTIAL: DID THEY SUGGEST CONNECTIONS TO OTHER INVESTORS OR RESOURCES?

DOCUMENTS SENT: (E.G., PITCH DECK, FINANCIALS) AND DATE SENT.

# NOTES & THOUGHTS

INVESTOR NAME:                                    DATE:

CONTACT INFORMATION:

PITCH METHOD: IN-PERSON    VIRTUAL    PHONE CALL    EMAIL

PITCH DURATION:

FOCUS AREA:

FUNDING SIZE:

PREVIOUS INVESTMENTS:

INTEREST LEVE: LOW    MEDIUM    HIGH

FOLLOW-UP ACTIONS:

FEEDBACK/QUESTIONS ASKED:

DECISION: ACCEPTED    DECLINED    PENDING

KEY TAKEAWAYS: INSIGHTS ABOUT THE INVESTOR OR THEIR PREFERENCES.

NETWORKING POTENTIAL: DID THEY SUGGEST CONNECTIONS TO OTHER INVESTORS OR RESOURCES?

DOCUMENTS SENT: (E.G., PITCH DECK, FINANCIALS) AND DATE SENT.

# NOTES & THOUGHTS

INVESTOR NAME:                                             DATE:

CONTACT INFORMATION:

PITCH METHOD: IN-PERSON    VIRTUAL    PHONE CALL    EMAIL

PITCH DURATION:

FOCUS AREA:

FUNDING SIZE:

PREVIOUS INVESTMENTS:

INTEREST LEVE: LOW    MEDIUM    HIGH

FOLLOW-UP ACTIONS:

FEEDBACK/QUESTIONS ASKED:

DECISION: ACCEPTED    DECLINED    PENDING

KEY TAKEAWAYS: INSIGHTS ABOUT THE INVESTOR OR THEIR PREFERENCES.

NETWORKING POTENTIAL: DID THEY SUGGEST CONNECTIONS TO OTHER INVESTORS OR RESOURCES?

DOCUMENTS SENT: (E.G., PITCH DECK, FINANCIALS) AND DATE SENT.

# NOTES & THOUGHTS

INVESTOR NAME:                                    DATE:

CONTACT INFORMATION:

PITCH METHOD: IN-PERSON    VIRTUAL    PHONE CALL    EMAIL

PITCH DURATION:

FOCUS AREA:

FUNDING SIZE:

PREVIOUS INVESTMENTS:

INTEREST LEVE: LOW    MEDIUM    HIGH

FOLLOW-UP ACTIONS:



FEEDBACK/QUESTIONS ASKED:



DECISION: ACCEPTED    DECLINED    PENDING

KEY TAKEAWAYS: INSIGHTS ABOUT THE INVESTOR OR THEIR PREFERENCES.



NETWORKING POTENTIAL: DID THEY SUGGEST CONNECTIONS TO OTHER INVESTORS OR RESOURCES?



DOCUMENTS SENT: (E.G., PITCH DECK, FINANCIALS) AND DATE SENT.

# NOTES & THOUGHTS

INVESTOR NAME:                                    DATE:

CONTACT INFORMATION:

PITCH METHOD: IN-PERSON     VIRTUAL     PHONE CALL     EMAIL

PITCH DURATION:

FOCUS AREA:

FUNDING SIZE:

PREVIOUS INVESTMENTS:

INTEREST LEVE: LOW     MEDIUM     HIGH

FOLLOW-UP ACTIONS:



FEEDBACK/QUESTIONS ASKED:



DECISION: ACCEPTED     DECLINED     PENDING

KEY TAKEAWAYS: INSIGHTS ABOUT THE INVESTOR OR THEIR PREFERENCES.



NETWORKING POTENTIAL: DID THEY SUGGEST CONNECTIONS TO OTHER INVESTORS OR RESOURCES?



DOCUMENTS SENT: (E.G., PITCH DECK, FINANCIALS) AND DATE SENT.

INVESTOR NAME:                                          DATE:

CONTACT INFORMATION:

PITCH METHOD: IN-PERSON    VIRTUAL    PHONE CALL    EMAIL

PITCH DURATION:

FOCUS AREA:

FUNDING SIZE:

PREVIOUS INVESTMENTS:

INTEREST LEVE: LOW    MEDIUM    HIGH

FOLLOW-UP ACTIONS:




FEEDBACK/QUESTIONS ASKED:




DECISION: ACCEPTED    DECLINED    PENDING

KEY TAKEAWAYS: INSIGHTS ABOUT THE INVESTOR OR THEIR
PREFERENCES.




NETWORKING POTENTIAL: DID THEY SUGGEST CONNECTIONS TO
OTHER INVESTORS OR RESOURCES?




DOCUMENTS SENT: (E.G., PITCH DECK, FINANCIALS) AND DATE SENT.

INVESTOR NAME:                                        DATE:

CONTACT INFORMATION:

PITCH METHOD: IN-PERSON    VIRTUAL    PHONE CALL    EMAIL

PITCH DURATION:

FOCUS AREA:

FUNDING SIZE:

PREVIOUS INVESTMENTS:

INTEREST LEVE: LOW    MEDIUM    HIGH

FOLLOW-UP ACTIONS:




FEEDBACK/QUESTIONS ASKED:




DECISION: ACCEPTED    DECLINED    PENDING

KEY TAKEAWAYS: INSIGHTS ABOUT THE INVESTOR OR THEIR PREFERENCES.




NETWORKING POTENTIAL: DID THEY SUGGEST CONNECTIONS TO OTHER INVESTORS OR RESOURCES?




DOCUMENTS SENT: (E.G., PITCH DECK, FINANCIALS) AND DATE SENT.

# NOTES & THOUGHTS

INVESTOR NAME:                                    DATE:

CONTACT INFORMATION:

PITCH METHOD: IN-PERSON    VIRTUAL    PHONE CALL    EMAIL

PITCH DURATION:

FOCUS AREA:

FUNDING SIZE:

PREVIOUS INVESTMENTS:

INTEREST LEVE: LOW    MEDIUM    HIGH

FOLLOW-UP ACTIONS:

FEEDBACK/QUESTIONS ASKED:

DECISION: ACCEPTED    DECLINED    PENDING

KEY TAKEAWAYS: INSIGHTS ABOUT THE INVESTOR OR THEIR PREFERENCES.

NETWORKING POTENTIAL: DID THEY SUGGEST CONNECTIONS TO OTHER INVESTORS OR RESOURCES?

DOCUMENTS SENT: (E.G., PITCH DECK, FINANCIALS) AND DATE SENT.

INVESTOR NAME: DATE:

CONTACT INFORMATION:

PITCH METHOD: IN-PERSON    VIRTUAL    PHONE CALL    EMAIL

PITCH DURATION:

FOCUS AREA:

FUNDING SIZE:

PREVIOUS INVESTMENTS:

INTEREST LEVE: LOW    MEDIUM    HIGH

FOLLOW-UP ACTIONS:



FEEDBACK/QUESTIONS ASKED:



DECISION: ACCEPTED    DECLINED    PENDING

KEY TAKEAWAYS: INSIGHTS ABOUT THE INVESTOR OR THEIR PREFERENCES.



NETWORKING POTENTIAL: DID THEY SUGGEST CONNECTIONS TO OTHER INVESTORS OR RESOURCES?



DOCUMENTS SENT: (E.G., PITCH DECK, FINANCIALS) AND DATE SENT.

INVESTOR NAME:                                        DATE:

CONTACT INFORMATION:

PITCH METHOD: IN-PERSON     VIRTUAL     PHONE CALL     EMAIL

PITCH DURATION:

FOCUS AREA:

FUNDING SIZE:

PREVIOUS INVESTMENTS:

INTEREST LEVE: LOW     MEDIUM     HIGH

FOLLOW-UP ACTIONS:


FEEDBACK/QUESTIONS ASKED:


DECISION: ACCEPTED     DECLINED     PENDING

KEY TAKEAWAYS: INSIGHTS ABOUT THE INVESTOR OR THEIR PREFERENCES.


NETWORKING POTENTIAL: DID THEY SUGGEST CONNECTIONS TO OTHER INVESTORS OR RESOURCES?


DOCUMENTS SENT: (E.G., PITCH DECK, FINANCIALS) AND DATE SENT.

# NOTES & THOUGHTS

INVESTOR NAME:                                    DATE:

CONTACT INFORMATION:

PITCH METHOD: IN-PERSON    VIRTUAL    PHONE CALL    EMAIL

PITCH DURATION:

FOCUS AREA:

FUNDING SIZE:

PREVIOUS INVESTMENTS:

INTEREST LEVE: LOW    MEDIUM    HIGH

FOLLOW-UP ACTIONS:

FEEDBACK/QUESTIONS ASKED:

DECISION: ACCEPTED    DECLINED    PENDING

KEY TAKEAWAYS: INSIGHTS ABOUT THE INVESTOR OR THEIR PREFERENCES.

NETWORKING POTENTIAL: DID THEY SUGGEST CONNECTIONS TO OTHER INVESTORS OR RESOURCES?

DOCUMENTS SENT: (E.G., PITCH DECK, FINANCIALS) AND DATE SENT.

# NOTES & THOUGHTS

INVESTOR NAME:                                                    DATE:

CONTACT INFORMATION:

PITCH METHOD: IN-PERSON    VIRTUAL    PHONE CALL    EMAIL

PITCH DURATION:

FOCUS AREA:

FUNDING SIZE:

PREVIOUS INVESTMENTS:

INTEREST LEVE: LOW    MEDIUM    HIGH

FOLLOW-UP ACTIONS:


FEEDBACK/QUESTIONS ASKED:


DECISION: ACCEPTED    DECLINED    PENDING

KEY TAKEAWAYS: INSIGHTS ABOUT THE INVESTOR OR THEIR PREFERENCES.


NETWORKING POTENTIAL: DID THEY SUGGEST CONNECTIONS TO OTHER INVESTORS OR RESOURCES?


DOCUMENTS SENT: (E.G., PITCH DECK, FINANCIALS) AND DATE SENT.

# NOTES & THOUGHTS

INVESTOR NAME:                                    DATE:

CONTACT INFORMATION:

PITCH METHOD: IN-PERSON    VIRTUAL    PHONE CALL    EMAIL

PITCH DURATION:

FOCUS AREA:

FUNDING SIZE:

PREVIOUS INVESTMENTS:

INTEREST LEVE: LOW    MEDIUM    HIGH

FOLLOW-UP ACTIONS:

FEEDBACK/QUESTIONS ASKED:

DECISION: ACCEPTED    DECLINED    PENDING

KEY TAKEAWAYS: INSIGHTS ABOUT THE INVESTOR OR THEIR PREFERENCES.

NETWORKING POTENTIAL: DID THEY SUGGEST CONNECTIONS TO OTHER INVESTORS OR RESOURCES?

DOCUMENTS SENT: (E.G., PITCH DECK, FINANCIALS) AND DATE SENT.

# NOTES & THOUGHTS

INVESTOR NAME:                                                    DATE:

CONTACT INFORMATION:

PITCH METHOD: IN-PERSON    VIRTUAL    PHONE CALL    EMAIL

PITCH DURATION:

FOCUS AREA:

FUNDING SIZE:

PREVIOUS INVESTMENTS:

INTEREST LEVE: LOW    MEDIUM    HIGH

FOLLOW-UP ACTIONS:




FEEDBACK/QUESTIONS ASKED:




DECISION: ACCEPTED    DECLINED    PENDING

KEY TAKEAWAYS: INSIGHTS ABOUT THE INVESTOR OR THEIR PREFERENCES.




NETWORKING POTENTIAL: DID THEY SUGGEST CONNECTIONS TO OTHER INVESTORS OR RESOURCES?




DOCUMENTS SENT: (E.G., PITCH DECK, FINANCIALS) AND DATE SENT.

# NOTES & THOUGHTS

INVESTOR NAME:                                 DATE:

CONTACT INFORMATION:

PITCH METHOD: IN-PERSON     VIRTUAL     PHONE CALL     EMAIL

PITCH DURATION:

FOCUS AREA:

FUNDING SIZE:

PREVIOUS INVESTMENTS:

INTEREST LEVE: LOW     MEDIUM     HIGH

FOLLOW-UP ACTIONS:

FEEDBACK/QUESTIONS ASKED:

DECISION: ACCEPTED     DECLINED     PENDING

KEY TAKEAWAYS: INSIGHTS ABOUT THE INVESTOR OR THEIR PREFERENCES.

NETWORKING POTENTIAL: DID THEY SUGGEST CONNECTIONS TO OTHER INVESTORS OR RESOURCES?

DOCUMENTS SENT: (E.G., PITCH DECK, FINANCIALS) AND DATE SENT.

# NOTES & THOUGHTS

INVESTOR NAME:                                             DATE:

CONTACT INFORMATION:

PITCH METHOD: IN-PERSON    VIRTUAL    PHONE CALL    EMAIL

PITCH DURATION:

FOCUS AREA:

FUNDING SIZE:

PREVIOUS INVESTMENTS:

INTEREST LEVE: LOW    MEDIUM    HIGH

FOLLOW-UP ACTIONS:


FEEDBACK/QUESTIONS ASKED:


DECISION: ACCEPTED    DECLINED    PENDING

KEY TAKEAWAYS: INSIGHTS ABOUT THE INVESTOR OR THEIR PREFERENCES.




NETWORKING POTENTIAL: DID THEY SUGGEST CONNECTIONS TO OTHER INVESTORS OR RESOURCES?




DOCUMENTS SENT: (E.G., PITCH DECK, FINANCIALS) AND DATE SENT.

# NOTES & THOUGHTS

INVESTOR NAME:                                        DATE:

CONTACT INFORMATION:

PITCH METHOD: IN-PERSON    VIRTUAL    PHONE CALL    EMAIL

PITCH DURATION:

FOCUS AREA:

FUNDING SIZE:

PREVIOUS INVESTMENTS:

INTEREST LEVE: LOW    MEDIUM    HIGH

FOLLOW-UP ACTIONS:


FEEDBACK/QUESTIONS ASKED:


DECISION: ACCEPTED    DECLINED    PENDING

KEY TAKEAWAYS: INSIGHTS ABOUT THE INVESTOR OR THEIR PREFERENCES.


NETWORKING POTENTIAL: DID THEY SUGGEST CONNECTIONS TO OTHER INVESTORS OR RESOURCES?


DOCUMENTS SENT: (E.G., PITCH DECK, FINANCIALS) AND DATE SENT.

# NOTES & THOUGHTS

INVESTOR NAME:                                                  DATE:

CONTACT INFORMATION:

PITCH METHOD: IN-PERSON     VIRTUAL     PHONE CALL     EMAIL

PITCH DURATION:

FOCUS AREA:

FUNDING SIZE:

PREVIOUS INVESTMENTS:

INTEREST LEVE: LOW     MEDIUM     HIGH

FOLLOW-UP ACTIONS:


FEEDBACK/QUESTIONS ASKED:


DECISION: ACCEPTED     DECLINED     PENDING

KEY TAKEAWAYS: INSIGHTS ABOUT THE INVESTOR OR THEIR PREFERENCES.


NETWORKING POTENTIAL: DID THEY SUGGEST CONNECTIONS TO OTHER INVESTORS OR RESOURCES?


DOCUMENTS SENT: (E.G., PITCH DECK, FINANCIALS) AND DATE SENT.

# NOTES & THOUGHTS

INVESTOR NAME:                                    DATE:

CONTACT INFORMATION:

PITCH METHOD: IN-PERSON    VIRTUAL    PHONE CALL    EMAIL

PITCH DURATION:

FOCUS AREA:

FUNDING SIZE:

PREVIOUS INVESTMENTS:

INTEREST LEVE: LOW    MEDIUM    HIGH

FOLLOW-UP ACTIONS:



FEEDBACK/QUESTIONS ASKED:



DECISION: ACCEPTED    DECLINED    PENDING

KEY TAKEAWAYS: INSIGHTS ABOUT THE INVESTOR OR THEIR PREFERENCES.




NETWORKING POTENTIAL: DID THEY SUGGEST CONNECTIONS TO OTHER INVESTORS OR RESOURCES?



DOCUMENTS SENT: (E.G., PITCH DECK, FINANCIALS) AND DATE SENT.

# NOTES & THOUGHTS

INVESTOR NAME:                                                  DATE:

CONTACT INFORMATION:

PITCH METHOD: IN-PERSON    VIRTUAL    PHONE CALL    EMAIL

PITCH DURATION:

FOCUS AREA:

FUNDING SIZE:

PREVIOUS INVESTMENTS:

INTEREST LEVE: LOW    MEDIUM    HIGH

FOLLOW-UP ACTIONS:




FEEDBACK/QUESTIONS ASKED:




DECISION: ACCEPTED    DECLINED    PENDING

KEY TAKEAWAYS: INSIGHTS ABOUT THE INVESTOR OR THEIR PREFERENCES.




NETWORKING POTENTIAL: DID THEY SUGGEST CONNECTIONS TO OTHER INVESTORS OR RESOURCES?




DOCUMENTS SENT: (E.G., PITCH DECK, FINANCIALS) AND DATE SENT.

# NOTES & THOUGHTS

INVESTOR NAME:                                    DATE:

CONTACT INFORMATION:

PITCH METHOD: IN-PERSON    VIRTUAL    PHONE CALL    EMAIL

PITCH DURATION:

FOCUS AREA:

FUNDING SIZE:

PREVIOUS INVESTMENTS:

INTEREST LEVE: LOW    MEDIUM    HIGH

FOLLOW-UP ACTIONS:




FEEDBACK/QUESTIONS ASKED:




DECISION: ACCEPTED    DECLINED    PENDING

KEY TAKEAWAYS: INSIGHTS ABOUT THE INVESTOR OR THEIR PREFERENCES.




NETWORKING POTENTIAL: DID THEY SUGGEST CONNECTIONS TO OTHER INVESTORS OR RESOURCES?




DOCUMENTS SENT: (E.G., PITCH DECK, FINANCIALS) AND DATE SENT.

# NOTES & THOUGHTS

INVESTOR NAME:                                        DATE:

CONTACT INFORMATION:

PITCH METHOD: IN-PERSON    VIRTUAL    PHONE CALL    EMAIL

PITCH DURATION:

FOCUS AREA:

FUNDING SIZE:

PREVIOUS INVESTMENTS:

INTEREST LEVE: LOW    MEDIUM    HIGH

FOLLOW-UP ACTIONS:


FEEDBACK/QUESTIONS ASKED:


DECISION: ACCEPTED    DECLINED    PENDING

KEY TAKEAWAYS: INSIGHTS ABOUT THE INVESTOR OR THEIR PREFERENCES.


NETWORKING POTENTIAL: DID THEY SUGGEST CONNECTIONS TO OTHER INVESTORS OR RESOURCES?


DOCUMENTS SENT: (E.G., PITCH DECK, FINANCIALS) AND DATE SENT.

# NOTES & THOUGHTS

INVESTOR NAME:                                         DATE:

CONTACT INFORMATION:

PITCH METHOD: IN-PERSON    VIRTUAL    PHONE CALL    EMAIL

PITCH DURATION:

FOCUS AREA:

FUNDING SIZE:

PREVIOUS INVESTMENTS:

INTEREST LEVE: LOW    MEDIUM    HIGH

FOLLOW-UP ACTIONS:


FEEDBACK/QUESTIONS ASKED:


DECISION: ACCEPTED    DECLINED    PENDING

KEY TAKEAWAYS: INSIGHTS ABOUT THE INVESTOR OR THEIR PREFERENCES.




NETWORKING POTENTIAL: DID THEY SUGGEST CONNECTIONS TO OTHER INVESTORS OR RESOURCES?


DOCUMENTS SENT: (E.G., PITCH DECK, FINANCIALS) AND DATE SENT.

INVESTOR NAME:                                         DATE:

CONTACT INFORMATION:

PITCH METHOD: IN-PERSON    VIRTUAL    PHONE CALL    EMAIL

PITCH DURATION:

FOCUS AREA:

FUNDING SIZE:

PREVIOUS INVESTMENTS:

INTEREST LEVE: LOW    MEDIUM    HIGH

FOLLOW-UP ACTIONS:




FEEDBACK/QUESTIONS ASKED:




DECISION: ACCEPTED    DECLINED    PENDING

KEY TAKEAWAYS: INSIGHTS ABOUT THE INVESTOR OR THEIR PREFERENCES.




NETWORKING POTENTIAL: DID THEY SUGGEST CONNECTIONS TO OTHER INVESTORS OR RESOURCES?




DOCUMENTS SENT: (E.G., PITCH DECK, FINANCIALS) AND DATE SENT.

# NOTES & THOUGHTS

INVESTOR NAME:                                         DATE:

CONTACT INFORMATION:

PITCH METHOD: IN-PERSON    VIRTUAL    PHONE CALL    EMAIL

PITCH DURATION:

FOCUS AREA:

FUNDING SIZE:

PREVIOUS INVESTMENTS:

INTEREST LEVE: LOW    MEDIUM    HIGH

FOLLOW-UP ACTIONS:


FEEDBACK/QUESTIONS ASKED:


DECISION: ACCEPTED    DECLINED    PENDING

KEY TAKEAWAYS: INSIGHTS ABOUT THE INVESTOR OR THEIR PREFERENCES.




NETWORKING POTENTIAL: DID THEY SUGGEST CONNECTIONS TO OTHER INVESTORS OR RESOURCES?




DOCUMENTS SENT: (E.G., PITCH DECK, FINANCIALS) AND DATE SENT.

# NOTES & THOUGHTS

INVESTOR NAME:                                          DATE:

CONTACT INFORMATION:

PITCH METHOD: IN-PERSON    VIRTUAL    PHONE CALL    EMAIL

PITCH DURATION:

FOCUS AREA:

FUNDING SIZE:

PREVIOUS INVESTMENTS:

INTEREST LEVE: LOW    MEDIUM    HIGH

FOLLOW-UP ACTIONS:



FEEDBACK/QUESTIONS ASKED:



DECISION: ACCEPTED    DECLINED    PENDING

KEY TAKEAWAYS: INSIGHTS ABOUT THE INVESTOR OR THEIR PREFERENCES.



NETWORKING POTENTIAL: DID THEY SUGGEST CONNECTIONS TO OTHER INVESTORS OR RESOURCES?



DOCUMENTS SENT: (E.G., PITCH DECK, FINANCIALS) AND DATE SENT.

# NOTES & THOUGHTS

# Pitch
# Dictionary

**accelerator**: a program to help startup founders speed up their growth by creating a small community of founders and providing them with the right people and resources(such as mentorship, sales, marketing, product design, research, etc.) to grow and scale their companies.

**angel**: an investor who individually provides capital to startups in exchange for convertible debt or equity stake(ownership) in the business.
accounts receivable (A/R): money owed to a company by its debtors.

**attrition rate**: the number of customers or employees you lose per year over the customers that you have. This number is show in a percentage. Example: If you have 1000 customers and you lose 200 this year, you will calculate 200/1000 = 0.2 which gives you an attrition rate of 20%.

**bootstrap**: solely using the profit from your startup to fund its growth.

**bottom line**: the company's net income.

**bridge note**: a short-term loan used to float a company between a pivot, major company change, or the next funding round is secured.

**burn rate**: the rate in which a business can operate before it runs out of money.

**business model**: a framework that explains the who, what, how, and why of a company which gives it the legs to become a successful company. Some Founders build out the business model before diving into the business plan.

**business plan**: a document displaying a company's goals, projected financials, and other future strategies and objectives.

**buyout**: the act of purchasing all ownership shares in a business.

**cap (valuation cap)**: the maximum price that your convertible note will convert into equity. It incentivizes the investor to invest early and lock them into a discount rate before growth.

**cap (capitalization) table**: a chart that lays out the ownership of all investors and what they invested to receive their ownership.

**capped convertible note**: an investment originally taken as a loan that has the option of converting into equity stake at a maximum valuation.

**cash flow**: the amount of cash flowing in and out of a business.

**churn rate**: for business with a subscription model, this is the percentage that people cancel or do not renew their subscription.

**close the round**: a point in which a founder stops taking new investment funding for their startup.

**cost of goods sold (COGS)**: the price for a founder/startup to produce a product or service including materials and labor.

**competitive advantage**: features and attributes of a business, product, or services that makes customers want to buy from that business versus its competitor(s).

**common stock (voting shares or ordinary shared)**: equity ownership in a company allowing the equity owner to vote on the election of board of directors and corporate policy .

**contingency**: a funding commitment made based on future results.

**conversion rate**: a metric that varies by company and product or service but leads to the percentage that a lead or customer is converted into a customer of a (another) product or service.

**convertible note (or convertible debt)**: a initial loan given by an investor. During the next round of investing, a third-party may then set the value of the startup business. The initial investor then has the option of converting that loan value into equity stake in the startup.

**crowdfunding**: a way to raise money through large groups of people (usually over the internet) in exchange for a product or service once the product or service has been launched.

**customer acquisition cost (CAC - /kak/)**: the sales and marketing cost related to turning a person into a customer.

**customer discovery**: a stage in product/service development where a company learns from the voice of the customer (VOC) how they can best produce or optimize their product/service. Customer discovery is usually conducted through phone calls, surveys, or focus groups.
Also see: Voice of the Customer (VOC)

**deal flow:** the process and rate in which an investment firm can intake new startups and provide them capital.

**design patents**: patents that cover the design or appearance of an invention. Usually valid for 14 years.

**dilution**: a decrease in founder, investor, and/or shareholder ownership/equity when a new investor provides funding or new shares are distributed.

**direct to consumer (D2C or DTC)**: a sells method where a brand provides their product to the end user/customer versus using a third-party retailer or distributor.

**earnings before interest, taxes, depreciation, and amortization (EBITDA)**: a measurement used by companies to track financial performance.

**equity (also known as equity stake, equity ownership, or equity percentage)**: the amount of ownership (usually in the form of a percentage) a person owns of a company.

**family office**: a privately owned wealth management group of wealth family members who invest in a variety of assets.

**fintech**: short for financial technology.

**friends and family round**: the initial stage of funding in which a founders asks people they know to invest into their company. Also see: pre-seed funding

**funding**: money provided for the growth of a business.
fund: a pool of money from multiple investors used for investment of one or more companies.

**gross income**: gross revenue minus cost of goods sold

**incubator**: a program to help startup founders create innovative products (usually technology related) by creating a small community of founders and providing them with the right people and resources (such as mentorship, sales, marketing, product design, research, etc.) to create their business model and companies.

**initial coin offering (ICO)**: a stage in a company's growth in which they raise funds using cryptocurrency.

**initial public offering (IPO)**: a stage in a company's growth in which they launch themselves as a company on the stock market.

**landed cost**: the total price of a product or shipment once it has arrived at a buyer's doorstep. The landed cost can include the original price of the product, transportation fees (both inland and ocean), customs, duties, taxes, tariffs, insurance, currency conversion, crating, handling and payment fees.

**letter of intent (LOI)**: a statement provided to a business by a customer show they they intend to be a customer in the near future depend certain stipulations such as fulfillment capabilities, logistics, and cost reduction.

**lifetime value (LTV) (average lifetime value)**: the revenue a customer brings in through the period in which they are a customer. Example: If a company's average customer used their $50/month subscription services for 5 years and that brought in revenue of $3,000, their lifetime value would be $3,000.

**line of business**: a division in a busines or industry focusing on a single product or group of similar products.

**margins (profit margins)**: the net income divided by net sales.

**market capitalization (market cap)**: the total value of all shares of stock a company possesses.

**material customer**: a consumer (usually a company) who consumes the largest amount (in revenue) of your products or services. They can either use, distribute, or sell your product to other consumers. Either way, it generates a large amount of revenue for the startup.

**mergers and acquisitions (M&A)**: the event which a company buys another and the two companies combine into one.

**micro loans**: A small loan provided by an individual or group of individuals that is not issued by a credit union or bank.

**minimum viable product (MVP)**: a product, service, or idea with just enough features to sell to a customer or test market feasibility.

**most favored nation (MFN)**: a country providing the most advantageous investment terms by another country.

**net income**: business sales minus cost of goods sold, general expenses, interest, and taxes.

**net sales**: the sum of a company's gross sales minus its discounts, allowances, and returns.

**oversubscribe**: when a founder has raised more money than what is needed or asked for during a particular funding round.

**patent pending**: a stage of the patent process where the patent has been filed. This puts the patent under temporary protection in case someone tries to "knock off" the product or file a patent for it. Investors have to keep in mind that only 52% of patents are actually approved.

**per-share earnings (EPS)**: a company's net profits divided by the number of common shares it has outstanding.

**perpetuity**: a return strategy that investors use that consists of a payback of a percentage or dollar amount for an indefinite period of time.

**pitch deck**: a brief presentation usually used by a founder that gives an overview of the business, it's traction, and/or it's progress. This document is used to secure funding.

**pre-seed funding**: the earliest stage of raising capital when a company has developed a minimal viable product (MVP) and has started testing the viability of the product.
Also see: friends and family round

**preferred stock**: equity ownership in a company that does not allow the owner to vote on corporate policy or electing members of the board of directors

**price-to-earnings (P/E) ratio**: the company's current share price relative to its per-share earnings (EPS).

**private equity**: a later stage of funding where a company raises funds to purchase a startup, small, medium, or large company that has not reached IPO.

**pro forma**: a detailed document providing financial projections based on confident assumptions about the company and market.

**proprietary**: related to ownership of a process or trade secret of the company.

**profit and loss (P&L)**: a financial document summarizing costs, expenses, and revenue acquired over a exact period of time.

**profit margin**: Profit Margin = (Net Profit / Revenue) * 100%

**quality of earnings (QoE)**: the accuracy, sustainability, and reliability of a company's earnings, indicating how well they reflect true economic performance rather than being influenced by accounting practices or non-recurring events.

**raise**: a short way of saying fundraise; an amount of money to be secured for startup investment.

**real estate investment trust (REIT)**: a funding vehicle owned by a publicly traded company who uses other people's capital to fund real estate projects.

**return on investment (R.O.I.)**: the ratio of net profit vs net cost that determines if a company or product is a smart financing decision. High R.O.I. means you made a smart decision while low R.O.I. means you did not make a intelligent decision or need to review ways to optimize profits and/or reduce cost.

**round**: the separate periods of funding that a startup goes through to valuate/re-valuate their company and raise more capital.
Also See: seed funding; pre-seed funding; friends and family round ; series A, series B, series C

**royalty**: a type of payback to investors that includes either a certain dollar amount or percentage that should be given back to the investor based on sales or net profit.

**run rate**: run rate is the forecast of sales or revenue based on a current period of financial data.

**runway**: the amount of money the business has on hand divided by its run rate – it tells you how long the business can continue its current trajectory without emptying the bank account.

**software as a service (SaaS)**: a business model where software is built using cloud computing and a third-party provider hosts the software for customers to use.

**seed funding (or seed capital)**: financing offered to the founder(s) of a company to help started their business.

**security**: a tradable financial asset such as a stock or bond.

**series A**: a company's first round of investment by Venture Capitalists and the second round of investment for startup funding.

**series B**: a company's second round of investment by Venture Capitalists and the third round of investment for startup funding.

**series C**: a company's third round of investment by Venture Capitalists and the fourth round of investment for startup funding.

**shares**: a representation of equity ownership of company that is broken down into units versus equity percentage.

**stock options**: for the protection of an investor, this gives an investor the ability to buy or sell a stock at an agreed upon amount and time.

**SWOT analysis**: a technique for evaluating the strengths, weaknesses, opportunities, and threats of a company.

**syndicate**: a group of investors pooling money together to fund a business.

**top line**: a company's gross sales or revenues.

**term sheet**: a high-level document outlining the business agreement between the founder and the investor.

**uncapped convertible note**: an investment originally taken as a loan that has the option of converting into equity stake at an unknown valuation.

**unicorn**: a business with +$1 billion valuation. Less than 0.07% of venture-backed companies maintain this status. There have been 39 unicorns since 2003 which it's about 4 companies every year.

**upfit (or fitout)**: is the tenant improvement work within an empty commercial shell space. The landlord typically provides HVAC and electrical services stubbed into the space, along with the separation walls between tenants- the rest is up to the renter and becomes the "tenant fitout".

**utility patents**: patents that cover the functional parts of an invention. Patents typically valid for 20 years.

**valuation**: the dollar amount in which a founder, investor, or analyst/appraiser estimates that a company is worth.

**value proposition (or value prop)**: a specific and sometimes unique benefit that a company delivers to it's customers through its product or service.

**venture capitalist (VC)**: a person or firm who invests time and/or money into company with the expectations of a high growth return.

**voice of the customer (VOC):** the process of finding out what a customer wants by asking the customer directly.

# Congratulations!

Look at all the progress you've documented! This tracker is now filled with insights, lessons, and milestones that reflect your hard work and growth. Each page tells the story of your journey...one pitch at a time.

As you move forward, use this knowledge to refine your approach, strengthen your relationships, and keep chasing your goals. You've come so far, and this is only the beginning.

Stay bold. Stay focused. Keep going.

The best is yet to come!

If you have any questions or would like to provide any feedback, please email us at Feedback@AfterThePitch.com and we'll be sure to get back to you.